I Eat Apples in Fall

by Mary Lindeen

first step nonfiction

Lerner Publications ◆ Minneapolis

LERNER

SOURCE™

Expand learning beyond the printed book. Download free, complementary educational resources for this book from our website, www.lerneresource.com.

The images in this book are used with the permission of: © sakkmesterke/Shutterstock.com, p. 4; © Catalin Petolea/Shutterstock.com, p. 5; © iStockphoto.com/Eric Michaud, p. 6; © iStockphoto.com/ fishwork, p. 7; © Sergey Borisov/Alamy, p. 8; © iStockphoto.com/RMAX, p. 9; © iStockphoto.com/ anandaBGD, p. 10; © moonlightbgd/Shutterstock.com, p. 11; © Maram/Shutterstock.com, p. 12; © Arina P Habich/Shutterstock.com, p. 13; © iStockphoto.com/pjohnson1, p. 14; © iStockphoto. com/aaron007, p. 15; © iStockphoto.com/milanfoto, p. 16; © Jo Kirchher/Getty Images, p. 17; © Joe Gough/Shutterstock.com, p. 18; © gkrphoto/Shutterstock.com, p. 19; © Andrey Starostin/Shutterstock. com, p. 20; © Klaus Vedfelt/Getty Images, p. 21; © Will Patton/DigitalVision/Getty Images, p. 22. Front cover: © iStockphoto.com/Kameleon007.

Main body text set in ITC Avant Garde Gothic Std Medium 21/25.
Typeface provided by International Typeface Corp.

Lerner Publications Company
A division of Lerner Publishing Group, Inc.
241 First Avenue North
Minneapolis, MN 55401 USA

For reading levels and more information, look up this title at www.lernerbooks.com.

Library of Congress Cataloging-in-Publication Data

Names: Lindeen, Mary, author.
Title: I eat apples in fall / by Mary Lindeen.
Description: Minneapolis : Lerner Publications, [2016] | Series: First step nonfiction. Observing fall | Audience: Ages 5–8. | Audience: K to grade 3. | Includes index.
Identifiers: LCCN 2015033973| ISBN 9781512407938 (lb : alk. paper) | ISBN 9781512412116 (pbk.) | ISBN 9781512409925 (ebook pdf)
Subjects: LCSH: Apples—Juvenile literature. | Autumn—Juvenile literature.
Classification: LCC SB363 .L544 2016 | DDC 634/.11—dc23
LC record available at http://lccn.loc.gov/2015033973

Manufactured in the United States of America
1 – CG – 7/15/16

Table of Contents

Picking Apples   4

Size   8

Color   11

Shape   15

Eating Apples   19

Glossary   23

Index   24

Picking Apples

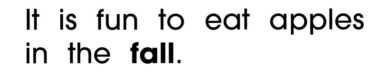

It is fun to eat apples in the **fall**.

An apple farm is called an orchard.

Apples grow on trees.

Apples are ready to **pick**
in the fall.

It is easy to pick an apple.
Just pull it off the tree!

Some apples are small.

Some apples are **tiny**.

Some apples are big!

Apples can be red.

Apples can be yellow.

Apples can be green.

The inside of an apple
is called the flesh.

The inside of an apple is
white. Apple seeds are
14 brown.

Apples are round.

These apple **slices** are circles.

The seeds in the middle
make a star.

A slice of apple pie looks
like a triangle. Yum!

Baked apples are warm and soft.

19

Apple chips are sweet and crunchy.

Apples are good for your brain, your heart, and your teeth.

Apples make great snacks any time of the year.

What is your favorite way to eat apples?

Glossary

fall – the season between summer and winter

pick – to collect or gather

slices – thin, flat pieces cut from something larger

tiny – very small

Index

apple chips – 20

apple pie – 18

baked apples – 19

fall – 4, 6

seeds – 14, 17

trees – 5, 7